INVISIBLE WITNESS

INVISIBLE WITNESS

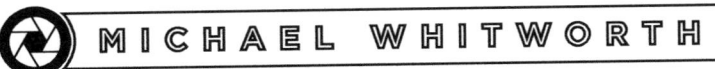

© 2019 by Michael Whitworth

All rights reserved. No part of this publication may be reproduced, stored in a retrieval system, or transmitted in any form or by any means without the prior written permission of the author. The only exception is brief quotations in printed reviews.

ISBN-10: 1944704426
ISBN-13: 978-1944704421

Published by Trail Press
Fort Worth, Texas 76244

Cover Design: Josh Feit, Evangela.com

All Scripture quotations are from The Holy Bible, English Standard Version®, copyright © 2001 by Crossway Bibles, a publishing ministry of Good News Publishers. Used by permission. All rights reserved.

acknowledgments

A very special thanks to the following people who made this book a reality:

Cody & Jaymie Archer, Mark & Lexie Bridges, Jeremy & Katie Gargis, Kent & Kim Horton, Denny & Susan Howell, Dale & Melanie Jenkins, Jeff & Laura Jenkins, Paul & Gail Norwood, Steve & Cheryl Orduño, Justin & Micah Paschall, and Jay & Linda Weaver.

All these contributed generously to this book's Kickstarter campaign. From the bottom of my heart, thank you!

To **Kristina Fortney** and **Rebecca Thompson**, two wonderful ladies who, independent of one another, inspired me to pick up a camera and search for the natural world's invisible witness. Look what the two of you started!

To my gracious and long-suffering wife **Sara** who first came along for the ride on many of my initial forays into creation, but as of late has stayed home more times than she wanted in order to raise our girls. She knows that, for me, photography is as much therapy as it is a hobby, and she has been incredibly supportive. I love you, Skippy.

Finally, to the Divine Artist, who each day dazzles me with a palette of colors that constantly speak to his glory.

Redwood National Park (top left)
Grand Canyon National Park (bottom left)

Death Valley National Park (top right)
Grand Teton National Park (bottom right)

the story so far…

In late 2006, I completed a brief commentary on Paul's Epistle to the Romans. For all of Romans' majesty, the one passage that made the greatest impact on me was the apostle's words in Romans 1:

> For what can be known about God is plain to them, because God has shown it to them. For his invisible attributes, namely, his eternal power and divine nature, have been clearly perceived, ever since the creation of the world, in the things that have been made.

The natural world is full of testimony to God's glory, Paul claims. Elsewhere, the apostle declared that God has not left himself "without witness" in the world (Acts 14:17).

Two things from my childhood left me with a love of the outdoors. First was my grandfather. Pop always embodied the weathered American cowboy to me; he was my personal Marlboro man. Trips to his house were spent camping, fishing, and hiking through the woods while pretending to be Davy Crockett. Pop taught me to sharpen a knife, whittle a spear, chop wood, make an alcohol stove, string a bow, start a fire, and a dozen other wilderness skills.

My time in Boy Scouts also fueled my wilderness wanderlust. Learning to navigate using a compass, landmarks, or the stars; selecting the right food for a long hike; packing the essentials and getting by with little else; discovering peace by embracing silence and solitude—these and more were the lessons I learned on the trail to Eagle. And after four years of college, a longing to "go outside" was reawakened within me by my study of the Book of Romans.

So in Summer 2007, I embarked on a rather epic road trip across the U.S. Totaling 9,150 miles, including 17 states and 12 national parks over 20 days, this road trip allowed me to see much of the American West. I was new to photography then, and though my pictures from that trip are by no means exceptional, each one is precious to me for what they represent—my first foray into discovering God's invisible witness to himself.

The initial trip took me across Texas to Big Bend National Park, then to Arizona to Saguaro and the north rim of the Grand Canyon, and then to Zion National Park, Death Valley, and Yosemite Valley.

After a brief detour up Highway 1 of the California coast to San Francisco, I visited Redwood and Crater Lake, and then the Olympic Peninsula of Washington State. After a long drive across Washington, Idaho, and Western Montana, I finished my trip with Glacier, Yellowstone, and Grand Teton before heading home.

Since then, I've been blessed to explore much more of America: her wilderness, her national parks, and the beauty endowed by her Creator. Each trip has taught me something about my beloved country, about myself—but most of all, about my Lord. Thank you for sharing this journey with me, a journey that bears witness to the invisible.

Road Trip Route

June 11-30, 2007

The Alamo
San Antonio, Texas

In November 2008, a business trip brought me to San Antonio. Since my early boyhood's obsession with Davy Crockett, the Alamo and its story have been well-known to me. Knowing that I'd be staying just a few blocks away, I naturally brought my camera along in hopes of capturing a decent shot of the famous mission.

The first night's photos were blah; a bald, colorless sky offered nothing. But on the second night, a storm had passed through downtown, and the clouds were a brilliant purple. I stood in front of the Alamo for over an hour, waiting for the perfect moment—the combination of gorgeous sunset color and no one standing in front of the mission.

That night was my first real experience with waiting.

Abraham Lincoln once said, "A man watches his pear tree day after day, impatient for the ripening of the fruit. Let him attempt to force the process, and he may spoil both fruit and tree. But let him patiently wait, and the ripe pear at length falls into his lap."

What was once a world of drive-thru fast food and Reader's Digest condensed book has morphed into something much worse. I don't do well at waiting: for service in a restaurant, for my latte in a coffee shop, or for my WiFi to stop misbehaving and reconnect me to the world wide web.

But patience is a biblical command (1 Thessalonians 5:14), a Christian virtue (2 Peter 1:6), and waiting is a spiritual experience (Isaiah 40:31). Landscape photography has made me an unwilling student, but learning to be better at waiting has made me a better person. Waiting forces me to slow down. To sit or stand. To be still. To look around. To enjoy what can't be appreciated while living life at warp speed.

Waiting. That, and Davy Crockett, are what I think of when I remember the Alamo.

Maroon Bells
Aspen, Colorado

The Maroon Bells near Aspen, Colorado are purported to be the most photographed peaks in North America, and I'd believe it. Both peaks are "fourteeners" and composed of mudstone that has hardened over time, giving the Bells their maroon-purple color.

I first visited the Maroon Bells in mid-August 2010 to backpack the loop around them with a friend. In late-September 2011, I returned to photograph the peaks in early morning light surrounded by fall colors. The blazing aspens along the interstate from Denver left me giddy with anticipation, and the scene the next morning did not disappoint.

The only thing that took away from the experience was how populated the viewpoint was that morning. Nearly 300,000 people visit the Bells during its very narrow season (July-September), so to say that it can be crowded is an understatement. I'm accustomed to arriving at a sunrise or sunset shoot an hour or so early to claim a good spot…but this proved almost too late at the Bells. One photographer had even erected a three-sided camouflaged canopy like one used by hunters to keep himself shielded from the cold. But it proved difficult for the rest of us to shoot around him. It was a major eye-roll, "Can you believe this guy?" moment.

It isn't often that I find myself in a crowded spot. When I do, I try to practice the Golden Rule and proper etiquette. **The outdoors are there for all of us, so there are occasions when you must share.** When you see a photographer shooting a scene, try not to get in the frame. If it's unavoidable because of close quarters, ask first before you step in front and take your own photograph. Most of us will be more than willing to let you jump in.

Unless it's early in the morning, it's super cold out, and we haven't had our coffee yet. Then all bets are off!

Panorama Point
Capitol Reef National Park

The Point Reyes
Point Reyes National Seashore

Mesa Arch
Canyonlands National Park

Acre for acre, Utah contains more iconic vistas and landmarks of the American West than any other state. My favorite area of Utah is Moab and its nearby national parks, Arches and Canyonlands, as well as Utah's Dead Horse Point State Park. Within the Island in the Sky section of Canyonlands is a natural arch known as Mesa Arch.

Mesa Arch is a popular sunrise location for photographers and tourists (in the summer, you must arrive at least an hour before sunrise to claim a decent spot). Below the arch is a five-hundred-foot sheer drop into Buck Canyon. Just before the sun crests the mountains to the east, the underside of the arch begins to grow brilliantly in shades of orange and red. When the sun first appears, the view will absolutely steal your breath away.

My first visit to Mesa was on my honeymoon in September 2009. I came away with a great shot of the glowing underside of the arch (opposite, top left), but my wife (using less photography experience and an inferior camera) came away with a better shot (opposite, top right). To say I felt outdone is an understatement!

My second visit wasn't for another seven years. In December 2016, I spent a few days in the Moab area, and the sun's position just before Winter Solstice provided a fantastic sun star (opposite, bottom).

But it's my latest visit, in July 2018, that has arguably been my favorite. Returning from a road trip to California and lodging one night in Moab, I rose early the next morning to drive out to the arch. While the summer sun was still too far north at its rise to provide a sun star, the color in the sky was incredible (opposite).

Collectively, Mesa Arch reminds me of the shifting seasons of life and time. Nothing is ever quite the same from one day to the next. I was twenty-two years old before I noticed that the sun does not rise and set in the same position each day. Beginning with the Summer Solstice, it makes its journey from the northern sky to the southern and then returns after the Winter Solstice. In my life "BP" (Before Photography), I assumed the sun rose due east and set due west everywhere and every day. But it doesn't.

And just as the sun never rises and sets the same way, the color of the sky is never the same. One day, it can be overcast and slate gray; the other, a brilliant kaleidoscope of hues never before witnessed. That's why I love returning to beautiful spots I've previously photographed. Each visit is varied; a new experience; a different blessing unique in its own way.

It's as if God makes each day unique for us. Habits and routines and the ebb and flow of domestic life might make each day seem the same, but **God beckons us from the routine to notice what makes each rotation of the earth special.** The sun shifts, the sky dazzles, and the underside of Mesa Arch glows a different shade of orange and red…

And all to the glory of a God who makes each day special.

Storm over the Green River
Canyonlands National Park

Dead Horse Point

Dead Horse Point State Park

There are some things you simply *must* do. You *have* to order deep dish pizza in Chicago or Tex-Mex in the Lone Star state. You *have* to go atop the Empire State Building in New York or shop Pikes Place market in Seattle. And when you visit Moab, you *must* hike to Delicate Arch.

What the magnolia flower is to Mississippi and the Lone Star is to Texas, Delicate Arch is to Utah. The sixty-foot sandstone arch adorns the state license plate and the postage stamp commemorating Utah's centennial in 1996. Delicate is the most famous of the two thousand arches located in Arches National Park.

To appreciate Delicate Arch up close requires you to hike the mile-and-a-half trail. I've visited Arches four times in the last decade and made the trek to Delicate on every occasion. The first and last were in winter, the second in autumn, and the third in spring. Each season offers a new perspective. In the spring, snow is still atop the La Sal Mountains in the background (left); in autumn, the sky is a more brilliant blue. But my favorite season is winter (right) when the sky has the most color.

Delicate Arch
Arches National Park

Fiery Furnace (previous)
Arches National Park

Turret Arch through North Window
Arches National Park

Other highlights of Arches include Balanced Rock, a natural stone monument rising to 128 feet. Balanced Rock is playing a losing game with gravity; eventually, the sandstone boulder (weighing 3,600 tons) atop the formation will tumble to the ground due to erosion. My first glimpse of Balanced Rock was of it silhouetted against the first light of a winter's morning (left).

But next to Delicate Arch, Arches' other "must-see" attraction is viewing Turret Arch through North Window. A trail from a parking lot leads to the Windows Section. Scrambling through North Window and up an opposing cliff, there is a precarious cleft in the rock just large enough for a photographer and a tripod. It's a tricky spot to get to, and I have a pair of jeans with a rip in the back pocket as a memento of my first visit.

Balanced Rock
Arches National Park

The second law of thermodynamics clearly explains that everything breaks down over time and trends towards entropy, and this becomes clearer with every visit I make to Arches. Formations that were intact at my last visit, I find collapsed on my return. Weather and erosion take their inevitable toll.

Indeed, Christianity understands that the entire universe is headed towards destruction. **And while creation bears witness to an invisible, benevolent Creator, that truth implies there is something beyond nature itself.** It cannot be worshiped, or else we miss the point of the natural world (cf. Romans 1:25).

My visits to Arches remind me of my Creator, that all of life points *to* him (Romans 11:36) and ends *before* him (Hebrews 9:27), and that, if not for the saving work of Christ (Romans 8:1), we all face certain ruin.

Behold, the Gospel according to Arches.

Queen Nefertiti Rock
Arches National Park

Pillars of the Earth
Arches National Park

If you believe, as I do, that the natural world bears witness to an invisible Father, no temple made by the hands of men or God can rival Yosemite. Located in California's High Sierras, Yosemite was the first of our national parks to be preserved from development; Abraham Lincoln signed legislation protecting Yosemite Valley in 1864, and the area became a national park in 1890.

Yosemite averages four to five million visitors a year, with most of them visiting Yosemite Valley, and it's little wonder why. Yosemite's massive granite domes and lush valley meadows; its roaring falls and splendid hiking trails offer up the best that God's creation has to offer.

Two famous personalities are virtually synonymous with Yosemite. The first is John Muir, the nineteenth-century conservationist who lobbied tirelessly to have Yosemite protected. Muir's time in the Sierras of California was translated into literature by his own hand and made him one of America's first travel writers. The second is Ansel Adams, the mid-twentieth century landscape photographer famous for his black-and-white shots of nature, and particularly Yosemite. There is a gallery in Yosemite Valley that features his work, and it is a must-see.

I first visited Yosemite on my summer road trip in 2007. I was new to photography then, and Yosemite proved a difficult place to shoot. Any landscape photographer quickly learns that the best times of day to grab great shots are at sunrise and sunset; there is usually little to be had at any other time.

Yosemite, however, is different. Especially since Yosemite Valley is surrounded by granite cliffs, the sun illuminates first one side of the valley, then the other, throughout the day. A waterfall will be in shadow in the morning; full light in the afternoon. On my first visit, I didn't know how to chase the sunlight through the valley. But in the gallery of Ansel Adams, I picked up a small book, a photography guide to Yosemite Valley to use "next time."

"Next time" wouldn't happen for another eleven years, but I returned in May 2018. Well in advance, I began planning where I would be and when in order to maximize my chances of getting the shots I wanted.

I would not be disappointed.

I narrowly avoided an unfortunate start to my visit. After a long day of travel, I arrived at my hotel and unloaded the car. The skies to the north were overcast, so I knew it was unlikely that I'd have a dramatic sunset at Tunnel View as I had planned. Plus, I was weary from travel, and it was over an hour's drive to Tunnel View from the hotel. A nap, a good meal, and an early bedtime were all tempting. But experience had taught me to go anyway, regardless of the weather forecast, and so I did. It proved to be a fantastic decision.

Yosemite Falls
Yosemite National Park

Tunnel View is, well, a beautiful scenic outlook over Yosemite Valley located just before you enter a long tunnel on the southern road to Oakhurst and Fresno. On my first visit in 2007, I had been unaware of the location until I was leaving; the shot I got (top left) was in the late afternoon (good) with a bald (bad) sky.

On my first night on my return trip, however, Tunnel View was clouded over as I had feared, but the sun behind me began to peak through and illuminate parts of the valley…and then… then… a rainbow (bottom left)! A real rainbow! I couldn't believe this blessing!

I lingered at Tunnel View, eating chili from my camp stove as I waited for the colors of dusk to settle in. A few moments after the sun dipped below the western peaks, the sky over Yosemite Valley shifted in shades of red and purple (right). It was magnificent—**sunsets after a storm can be the most dramatic!**

Tunnel View
Yosemite National Park

The next day took me to the base of Lower Yosemite Falls and to Cathedral Beach to experience the morning light in the valley. Lower Yosemite Falls is the final 320-foot drop of three cascades that make up Yosemite Falls. Long ago, the Native American tribe known as the Ahwahneechee founded their main village at the base of these falls. Like all the waterfalls in Yosemite, the flow of these falls is strongest in springtime because of the snowmelt; by mid-summer, the flow has slowed to barely a trickle.

Cathedral Beach is a lovely picnic spot along the banks of the Merced River with Yosemite's famed El Capitan looming large. On this particular morning, I was blessed to find a small pool reflecting El Capitan; when I returned to the spot the next day, the pool had already evaporated. It was a reminder of the importance of taking advantage of every one of life's opportunities as they come our way; those same chances might not exist tomorrow!

But the highlight of my first full day on this Yosemite trip was venturing up to Glacier Point and its views of Yosemite Valley, dominated by Half Dome. Glacier Point rises 3,200 feet above the valley floor (over 7,200 feet in total elevation). Because of snow, the road to Glacier Point usually is open only from late-May to October, but it had opened early this particular year.

Though Glacier Point offers a breathtaking view of Yosemite Valley, Tenaya Canyon, and Vernal and Nevada Falls, the first landmark everyone notices is Half Dome (elevation 8,844 feet), a granite dome that appears to have been cut in half. Half Dome is a popular climb, but reaching the top requires the use of steel cables towards the end and is certainly not for the faint of heart.

Half Dome
Yosemite National Park

Panorama at Glacier Point
Yosemite National Park

Half Dome from Glacier Point
Yosemite National Park

Being deathly afraid of heights, I was content to admire Half Dome from the other side of the valley. I arrived more than three hours before sunset because I wanted to watch the light change across Half Dome's face, and I was not disappointed. Dramatic clouds gave way to shifting colors of blue and pink as dusk descended.

Once it was pitch black, I returned to my car for some supper and a nap, setting an alarm for 10:30 pm, at which point I returned to the overlook to photograph the rise of the Milky Way over Half Dome (bottom left).

The sight was thrilling.

Watching the rise of the Milky Way requires a lot of things to fall into place. First, you have to be at a location with no light pollution (that is, nowhere near civilization). You also need clear skies and no moon.

All these came together for me that night at Half Dome (it was well after midnight before I returned to my hotel, but it was totally worth it).

The next evening, I made a return to Mirror Lake, a site I had visited on my previous trip to Yosemite. Mirror Lake is at the end of a mile-long trail in Yosemite Valley and is my favorite spot. Standing watch over the lake is Mount Watkins, and it is fed by Tenaya Creek, though the lake's water level is never very high (it reaches its peak with the spring runoff).

My return to Mirror Lake again gave me an opportunity to compare my growth as a photographer. I had just started to dabble in photography when I first laid eyes on the lake; now, I had eleven years' experience under my belt. Comparing the two photos—taken from the same spot, just eleven years apart—several things jump out at me.

Yes, I'm using a higher-quality camera and lens. But this isn't the only thing that makes the second photo better. Time of day matters; the second was taken in the late afternoon when the scene was not washed out. Time of year matters; the first photograph was taken in June; the second in May when the water level is higher and the reflection better. The composition is better; I've exchanged a boulder on the left for a large tree limb.

Mirror Lake
Yosemite National Park

Altogether, this second trip to Yosemite ranks among the best of my photographic experiences because **I was impressed with the impulse to worship that Yosemite triggered within me.** Whenever I'm at an overlook for sunrise or sunset, I often find myself singing hymns to pass the time. Soon, what begins as a subconscious humming to myself gives way to passionate (if not audible) praise. Perched atop a boulder at Mirror Lake, I worshiped. Watching the day's last light burn the face of Half Dome, I worshiped. Witnessing a double rainbow at Tunnel View, I worshiped.

I remember leaving Yosemite on my initial visit with one passage on my heart: "Praise the LORD! Praise God in his sanctuary; praise him in his mighty heavens! Praise him for his mighty deeds; praise him according to his excellent greatness! […] Let everything that has breath praise the LORD! Praise the LORD!" (Psalm 150:1-2, 6). That passage was again on my lips when I returned.

For all the temples and sanctuaries made by the hands of God or men, none inspires worship in my heart like the beauty of Yosemite.

Cathedral Beach
Yosemite National Park

Wind Canyon Overlook
Theodore Roosevelt National Park

Since the unexpected deaths of my dad and son, Father's Day has always been a difficult day. Grief always seems to hijack the day we have set aside to honor dads. So in 2018, when my wife asked what I wanted for Father's Day, I told her, "Honestly, to go away somewhere and pretend the day doesn't exist." "Done," she said, and with her blessing, I planned an epic week-long camping trip to the Dakotas, two states I'd never visited.

The first day of my trip was nothing but slate-gray overcast skies and then dreary, drizzly rain. The landscape in Wind Cave National Park resembled a blurry watercolor painting, and as I looked to my next destination—Devil's Tower, Wyoming—the forecast was the same. So I called an audible and headed north to South Dakota's northern twin.

Theodore Roosevelt was the second national park on my itinerary. Frankly, I wasn't expecting much in the way of beauty. For the second straight day in the Dakotas, the sunset was rained out, and I began to despair that the entire trip would be a waste. But on Tuesday evening, at Wind Canyon Overlook, the divine Artist put on a show!

Our twenty-sixth president, for whom the park is named, once said that had it not been for the time he spent in North Dakota as a young man, he would have never been president. I came to appreciate what he meant. It reminded me of a poor man's Yellowstone; it had much of the scenery and wildlife of Yellowstone, but without the crowds.

As I stood at Wind Canyon Overlook, a bluff offering a dramatic view of the meandering Little Missouri River, I watched the sky's tones shift from blue to yellow to orange to fiery red. I thought about my grief, the losses of my father and my son. I thought about the previous two consecutive sunsets I'd missed because of overcast skies. And all this made this particular sunset at Wind Canyon more meaningful.

We can sometimes become consumed by all that is amiss in our life and easily blame God for our problems. But lest we become obsessed with what we've missed out on, the Lord has an uncanny way of calling us to turn aside and notice the great beauty that remains in the world. Has life become an endless series of overcast skies and slate-gray sunsets? Hold on until tomorrow. God might set the sky on fire with his glory…just for you.

Parker Group
Sequoia National Park

Lady Bird Johnson Grove
Redwood National Park

Every so often in our national parks, I stumble upon things that defy imagination. My two favorite attractions in America's natural freak show are the giant redwoods and sequoias of California. Some of the best photographs from my initial road trip were from Redwood National Park. The towering redwoods were shrouded by mist and fog, which only added to the surreal aura of the place. In one clearing, I decided to set up my tripod just high enough off the ground to allow me to lay under it, flat on my back, and aim my camera straight up to capture these natural towers.

The average redwood height is about 360 feet, and sequoias slightly less. The *tallest* tree in the world, a redwood known as Hyperion, tops off at 380 feet, and the world's *most massive* tree is Sequoia's General Sherman Tree, possessing a diameter at its base of 36 feet.

As massive as these trees are, however, they fall far short of tickling the feet of the Almighty. They remind us that the greatest things of the natural world are but specks in the eyes of the Lord; and that, while these trees were created on the third day, it was only after God had created the first man and woman on the sixth that he declared creation to be "very good." You and I, then, mean more to God than the grandest of his grand designs.

Upper Antelope Canyon
Page, Arizona

Desert Sunset

Saguaro National Park

Horseshoe Bend
Page, Arizona

In August 2017, a business trip took me to Arizona, and once I was done with work, at the top of my list was Horseshoe Bend, a serpentine turn in the Colorado River a few miles south of Page. It's a popular tourist stop in the summer; there are no railings and the drop from the cliffs is pretty precarious. If you do a Google search, you'll see that several images of the bend contain the entirety of the river at the bottom of the shot. But getting this shot requires nerves and a comfort with heights I just don't possess!

I could not have asked for or imagined a more perfect sunset. The clouds. The color. I spent about two hours at this location, waiting for the light to be just right, and I wasn't disappointed. At the time, it had been quite a while since I had photographed a sunset this perfect. It was as if everything came together.

Sometimes, things in life come together in such a way that you can't help but offer thanks for God's blessing and goodness. The world may call these moments of random serendipity, but the people of God know better.

Engaging conversation over good coffee. The giggle of a small child. An epic hike through mountain meadows. The sound of rain on the roof while curled up with a good book. And yes, a sunset's light from atop steep canyon walls. All these offer us a glimpse at the face of a smiling Father who delights in his creation. And what some consider random, I believe are intentional acts inspired by a God who loves to be found in the oddest places.

As I get older, I realize these days when "things just come together" are few and far between. Life is hard. Bad days happen. Like the little boy Alexander in the beloved children's book, I've more than once packed my bags for Australia.

But God has an uncanny way of capping a string of rough days with a very good one. So whenever things have been tough of late, I go out of my way to remain sensitive to the little things God might be doing to lift my spirits and reveal his smile. On this Sunday night in August at Horseshoe Bend, he did so with a spectacular sunset.

Hyggeligt.

It's a Danish word with no solid English equivalent. It refers to "a feeling of extreme comfort or coziness." You experience *hyggeligt* when you're filled with warmth while surrounded by friends and family for the holidays. Or snuggled up to that special someone by the fire, watching a movie.

It's what I feel when I photograph waterfalls.

There's a degree of difficulty in shooting waterfalls. They look terrible in midday light; you want to do so early in the morning, late in the day, or (best!) when it's overcast. You also have to be careful about spray from the falls getting your camera gear soaked. But the biggest obstacle was learning to slow the shutter speed down to achieve a nice silky effect for the water itself. A shutter that's too fast will freeze the water in mid-air; one that's too slow will pick up motion blur from nearby leaves and other fragile things.

Toketee Falls
Umpqua National Forest, Oregon

Clearwater Falls
Umpqua National Forest, Oregon

Multnomah Falls
Columbia River Gorge, Oregon

For any lover of waterfalls, the Pacific Northwest is Mecca. There is a website dedicated to cataloging all the waterfalls in the Northern California/Oregon/Washington area, and it's proven to be a great help to me whenever I have the itch.

I think about a lot as I stand at a high point looking down on or at the base of the falls looking up. I think about the roar of the falls, how the noise drowns all else out, and it has the odd effect of quieting your mind.

I think about how the waterfall is never the same from one day to the next. The water is different; the droplets that passed by yesterday aren't the same as those today, but in a way they are. Because of erosion and other effects, the falls aren't technically the same from one year to the next, but in a way they are.

Lemolo (left) and Whitehorse (right) Falls
Umpqua National Forest, Oregon

As ridiculous as it sounds, I think about the fear I'd feel if I were a water droplet going over the falls. I'm terrified of heights. But even though it's dangerous, reason says the falls pose no threat to water. It's the same at the bottom as it was at the top.

I've fallen a lot in life. Sometimes, because of mistakes I've made. Sometimes, because of tragedy. Sometimes, because of mistreatment from others. God, however, has always been immensely faithful to me when I've fallen.

The child of God never has need to fear a fall, for God is faithful to see us through it, ensuring that we are the same at the bottom as we were at the top. The fall will not change us, but in a way it will, and for the better.

And like a waterfall, tough times will drown out the insignificant noise of life and cause you to focus on the beauty and wonder that has always been around you. Sometimes you can't hear Him speak until the Roar drowns out all else.

Christine Falls
Mount Rainier National Park

Sol Duc Falls

Olympic National Park

Sawtooth Range
Stanley, Idaho

You know those personality tests you see in magazines or on Facebook? Coke or Pepsi? Coffee or tea? Well done or rare? Mountains or beach? I'll confess that I'm hands down a mountain person. In fact, any day I spend at the beach is, to me, a wasted day that I could have been in the mountains somewhere.

And I have rather strong opinions about mountains. Growing up in the Deep South, the Smokies were the closest thing I knew to mountains. Woodall Mountain in the northeast corner of my native state of Mississippi rises to a pitiful 806 feet above sea level, and Cheaha Mountain in my adopted state of Alabama is only 2,407 feet.

Perhaps I got the fever for mountains when, at less than a year old, my parents took me to visit Colorado. Growing up, on our shelf at home was a painted rock, a souvenir from our visit to Pikes Peak (elevation 14,114 feet). Maybe the fever was reawakened when I was fifteen and visited Denver; I'll never forget my first sight of the sunset over the Front Range.

Nothing else in all of God's natural creation steals my breath away like mountains. My pulse quickens. The adrenaline releases. Something deep in my soul stirs to life when peaks come into view. Now that I think about, my attachment to mountains borders on the romantic.

From the beginning of civilization, all peoples have associated mountains with the presence of deity. Ancient cultures in Syria and Palestine believed the gods inhabited Mount Hermon (elevation 9,232 feet) on the Syrian-Lebanon border. The Greeks had Olympus (9,573 feet), and the Jews, Sinai (7,497 feet). Even today, Everest (29,029 feet), K2 (28,251 feet), and Kilimanjaro (19,341 feet) inspire awe like nothing else.

Chugach Mountains
Glen Highway, Alaska

Superstition Mountains
Apache Junction, Arizona

I've camped very close to Mount Denali, the highest peak in North America (20,310 feet), and stood at the base of California's Mount Whitney, the highest point in the lower 48 (14,505 feet). But my favorite mountain is Washington's Mount Rainier (14,411 feet). On a clear day, you can see the peak prominently from downtown Seattle, but nothing rivals its beauty up close.

I had visited the Seattle-area several times and admired Rainier from a distance but had never been able to visit until a speaking trip in July 2018. I rose at 3:00 am in my hotel to make the drive out to Reflection Lake, an aptly-named body of water to the south of Rainier's mighty peak. The water was like glass, and the reflection mirror-like that morning. I've found that few things in life live up to the hype, but Mount Rainier in all its glory is one of them. One of Rainier's attractions is the famed Wonderland Trail, a ninety-three-mile hiking path that encompasses the mountain.

You better believe that hiking Wonderland is on my life's bucket list.

Skyline from Kerry Park
Seattle, Washington

Like the ancients, mountains point me to the divine, but not because I believe God is there versus somewhere else. It's because the mountains remind me of my smallness and God's greatness. As a child, I often heard Psalm 121:1 quoted, "I lift up my eyes to the hills. From where does my help come? My help comes from the LORD, who made heaven and earth." For a long time, I mistakenly thought the psalmist was claiming his help came from the mountains (which is what the King James Version suggests). But as other translations render it, the first part is indeed a question.

Unlike the ancients, the psalmist knew that mountains held no special power, and this theme runs throughout all of Scripture. During the Flood, the highest peak was submerged by about twenty feet (Genesis 7:19-20), and Psalms also claims that mountains tremble and quake at God's presence (Psalm 18:7). **Thus, whenever I behold the mountains of the earth, I'm reminded of the utter sovereignty of God, of his kingship over the universe, of how nothing is beyond his control.** As mighty and immovable and unforgiving as a mountain may seem, they melt like wax before the Lord (Micah 1:4). And in turn, no matter the obstacles in life's path, though they may be mountain-sized, faith in God can tell such mountains to take a swim in the ocean (Mark 11:23).

Oh, and I prefer Coke; Pepsi is of the devil. I like both coffee *and* tea. And I'll take my steak medium.

Reflection Lake
Mount Rainier National Park

Oxbow Bend

Grand Teton National Park

If mountains are my favorite landscape, and Rainier my favorite mountain, the Grand Tetons are surely my favorite mountain *range*. My first visit to the Tetons came at the tail end of my 2007 road trip. I was road weary, and what was supposed to be a three-night stay became a brief mid-day visit before starting for home early.

But it had nothing to do with the view. The Tetons were mesmerizing. I couldn't look away. I was immediately impressed with how close they are to the road. Unlike many mountain ranges, the Tetons have no foothills. They're just there.

Homesick as I was, I couldn't wait to return, and I got my opportunity in September 2011. I timed my visit for the peak of fall colors in Jackson Hole, and I wasn't disappointed. I remember how fiercely ablaze with color the aspens were along the roadside.

On my brief first visit, I actually came away with the best shot of my trip, one of Oxbow Bend and Mount Moran in the background with two kayakers in the foreground unwittingly providing a grand sense of scale to the scene. Arriving late in the day on my second visit, I made a beeline for Oxbow Bend again just in time for a beautiful lavender sunset.

Next on my list of "must-see" places was Snake River Overlook. This site was made famous by Ansel Adams and his now-iconic photograph of the scene.

In it, the s-curve of the Snake River offers terrific composition in the shadow of the Teton Range. In the sky above the range is a clearing storm at sunset.

It's my favorite Ansel Adams photograph.

My first morning in Jackson Hole, guess where I headed for sunrise? The rising sun illuminating the peaks and the fall colors of the trees along the river bank combined for yet another stunning painting on the canvas of the Divine Artist.

On my third visit to the Tetons some nine months later, I returned to the same place and witnessed a beautiful pink color on the highest peak just before sunrise, with dramatic dawn clouds looming above.

Snake River Overlook
Grand Teton National Park

But there is more to the Tetons than Oxbow Bend and Snake River Overlook. On another morning during my second visit, I set up with a row of fellow photographers to shoot what is arguably the most photographed barn in America, an old barn in a place called Mormon Row. The print has adorned the wall of my dining room ever since.

My first visit to the Tetons was too brief because I was too weary. But both of my subsequent visits have been refreshing for my soul in multiple ways. All of us need "that place" in our lives that offers refreshment and refuge.

In the Old Testament, David wrote more than a few psalms from the Cave of Adullam, a place of refuge when on the run from jealous King Saul. From this cave, he once wrote, "Be merciful to me, O God, be merciful to me, for in you my soul takes refuge; in the shadow of your wings I will take refuge, till the storms of destruction pass by. I cry out to God Most High, to God who fulfills his purpose for me" (Psalm 57:1-2).

Elijah, too, was directed to Mount Sinai to have his spirit and ministry refreshed. In the New Testament, Jesus often escaped into the wilderness to reconnect with the Father. **The mountains refresh me, and none more so than the Tetons. There, I am reminded in whom my faith lies, receive assurance of his love, and am refreshed for what lies ahead.** David's final line of Psalm 57 always comes to mind when I leave the mountains, and particularly the Tetons: "Be exalted, O God, above the heavens! Let your glory be over all the earth!"

Mormon Barn (previous page)
Grand Teton National Park

Chapel of the Transfiguration
Grand Teton National Park

Oxbow Bend in Autumn
Grand Teton National Park

Schwabacher Landing
Grand Teton National Park

Sunset at Toroweap Overlook
Grand Canyon National Park

There are few unwritten, hard-and-fast rules in life. One of them is Murphy's Law: Everything that can go wrong will go wrong at the worst possible time and in the worst possible way. Another is that you will never find what you are looking for—until you no longer need it. A watched pot never boils. There's nothing new under the sun—or on television, for that matter. You don't wear white after Labor Day or to a wedding. Never ask a woman if she's pregnant.

Perhaps the most depressing of these rules is that few things in life live up to their hype. But the Grand Canyon is one of them. I tell everyone I know who goes on a road trip out west: "Go to the Grand Canyon; you won't regret it."

An average of six million people visit this massive ditch in northern Arizona every year, and while there are more visitors to Great Smoky Mountain National Park (eleven million), you won't find as many international visitors there as you will at the Grand Canyon. When people from around the world visit the U.S., they feel like they *must* visit the Grand Canyon. And there's no wonder why.

I visited the Grand Canyon's South Rim as a boy with my family during summer vacation, and my mom's diligent scrap-booking preserved the photos of that trip. So on my road trip in 2007, I planned to visit the North Rim. The North Rim's Cape Royal and Bright Angel Point offer fantastic views of the canyon; the North Rim is, in fact, my favorite of the two rims. It's cooler (due to its higher elevation) and less populated (due to it being out of the way).

One is struck by the immense stillness and sacredness of the Grand Canyon. At the overlooks at sunrise (less so at sunset), the silence can be deafening. Sometimes, the only sound is the wind, the call of a crow, or your own breath.

Bright Angel Point (next page)
Grand Canyon National Park

On our honeymoon, my wife and I made the North Rim our first stop; we both soaked up the quietness of the place as we witnessed a brilliant sunset that I have never seen paralleled in my six visits.

If the mountains refresh my soul and Yosemite inspires worship, the Grand Canyon never fails to evoke in me a sense of awe and wonder. **As we transition from childhood to adulthood, we all lose our sense of wonder about the world around us. It's inevitable.** But the Grand Canyon helps us recapture that. You stand on the rim and gaze upon the vast emptiness; it's always pretty unbelievable.

More unbelievable? That we are expected to believe this grand ditch was created solely by water over millions of years. No, I prefer the narrative that God drug his fingertip through the mud and rock at some point in the very distant past. In fact, if you squint and look long enough at this grand canyon's walls, you can still make out his fingerprints—

Still bearing witness to the glory of an invisible God.

Point Imperial (top), Cape Royal (bottom, opposite)
Grand Canyon National Park

Sunrise from Mather Point
Grand Canyon National Park

Sunrise from Yaki Point
Grand Canyon National Park

The Watchman (bottom left)
Zion National Park

The Subway (bottom right)
Towers of the Virgin (top)
Zion National Park

Just a few hours' drive to the northwest of the Grand Canyon's North Rim is Zion National Park. In some ways, Zion is the opposite of the Grand Canyon. Whereas at the latter you are on the top looking down into the canyon, in Zion, you are at the bottom looking up.

The fifteen-mile-long Zion Canyon, the main part of the park, was settled by Mormons in the 1860s. The names of many of the landmarks and sites retain the Mormon influence in the area (e.g., Court of the Patriarchs, Angel's Landing, Mount Moroni, Kolob Canyon).

I first visited Zion on my 2007 road trip and eagerly returned with my wife two years later on our honeymoon. One of the highlights of that visit was hiking the Narrows in Zion Canyon. Springdale, the gateway town to Zion National Park, offers an abundance of fantastic restaurants (order the made-from-scratch carrot cake at Oscar's; thank me later).

The Narrows
Zion National Park

A disappointment of that honeymoon visit, however, was failure to reach the Subway, a fork of the Virgin River where flash-floods have eroded the rock to resemble an underground subway tunnel. The hike is a strenuous one, and we left too late in the morning to make it to the Subway and back before dark. "Next time," I resolved. Next time, I would come prepared. That "next time" came two years later. At the top of my agenda was hiking to the Subway. My wife and I secured a permit early in the morning and hit the trail on time, determined to hike as quickly as possible. The route to the Subway requires climbing about four hundred feet down the side of a cliff into the canyon and then hiking upstream, crossing and recrossing the river several times, and scrambling up and over more than a few boulders. After nearly four hours of hiking, we made it to the Subway, and it did not disappoint. The turquoise hue of the deep pools contrasted nicely with the rock walls. We spent about an hour photographing the scene before returning to the trailhead—which, at the end, requires climbing up the aforementioned four-hundred-foot cliff!

My visits to Zion always remind me of a unique, yet important, truth about the natural world around us: **that our spirituality is bound up in the land.** I don't mean this in a way reflected in Asian or Native American religions. But it is biblical to say that the land teaches us to rely on and connect with God. One of the best books I've ever read, *The Bible and the Land* by Gary Burge, opened my eyes to this reality in Scripture (cf. Deuteronomy 8:7-18).

When the Mormons came to Zion, they bestowed on it names from the Bible. Their faith was strengthened by their connection to the land. I have a friend who is a farmer, and in his nearly eighty years, he's come to believe that things went a little off the rails morally in our culture when we became less dependent on the land; i.e., when farmers became factory workers and the entire world industrialized. He may be on to something. Many of the farmers I've known knew how to trust God better than I; they knew what it was like to pray for "daily bread."

The hike to the Subway isn't so much dangerous as it is long and exhausting. I've prayed for safety every time. I felt the Lord's blessing every time. Who knew that a simple hike could prompt prayer and faith, reflection and blessing? You and I, as spiritual creatures, were made to be bound up in the land.

The Subway
Zion National Park

Sunrise over Zabriskie Point
Death Valley National Park

Toroweap Overlook
Grand Canyon National Park

From time to time, photography takes me far beyond the boundaries of civilization—a place where warm, soft beds, electricity, and (worst of all) cell service do not exist.

The Grand Canyon overlook known as Toroweap is sixty miles from the nearest paved road. Traversing the road requires a high-clearance four-wheel-drive vehicle and takes nearly three hours to complete. Only a few primitive campsites exist near the overlook and require a permit in advance. Visiting Toroweap had been on my bucket list for several years, and I wasn't disappointed when I arrived.

So far removed from anything urban, Toroweap forces you to slow down. Take your time. See what's really in front of you. Nothing can be rushed here. Sitting out at the overlook, awaiting sunset or sunrise, affords one a lot of time to think and reflect. To allow the mind to wander. And wonder. At the magnificence of this canyon that we have rightly designated "Grand." At the skill of the Creator in crafting this natural temple to his glory. At how small an individual is in the grand scheme of things.

I shot the sunset with an ex-Marine from Phoenix who had an old-school photo rig. While I was shooting digital and could rattle off hundreds or thousands of shots to a memory card, he could only take a handful of photographs on film. He had to be careful with each one. He told me, "Most people come out here and don't really look at what's in front of them. They set their camera up, take a bunch of shots very quickly. Stand around and look at their phones while they wait for sunset. But you can't do that. You have to be patient. You have to look up. You have to pay attention to what the light is doing."

Toroweap offers a cure to what ails many of us. Be patient. Look up. Pay attention to what the Light is doing. As my daddy used to say, "That'll preach."

"Be still, and know that I am God" (Psalm 46:10).

The Wave
Coyote Buttes, Paria Canyon-Vermilion Cliffs Wilderness

Halfway between Kanab, Utah and Page, Arizona, lies Coyote Buttes and a very small area known as "The Wave." Access to the Wave is limited to just twenty people per day, and this restriction is rigorously enforced. It is a federally-designated wilderness area, and trespassers face stiff fines and prosecuted in federal court. Sheriffs and rangers patrol the area and ask to see permits from every hiker. Permits must be obtained online via a lottery that runs four months before the desired date. More than 160,000 people apply for permits per year; less than 7,500 are selected.

Even with a permit, the Wave is a bit of a challenge to access. The hike is six miles round-trip, and there is no trail—one must hike cross-country. Rangers knock over cairns and other markers; the only "path" discernible is footprints left in sandy areas. Plus, it can be scorching, and one must carry a minimum of three liters of water. So why would 160,000 people try so hard to visit the Wave?

You likely have seen pictures of the Wave; it's been popular in screensavers for years. The lines in the rock create gorgeous patterns that are unlike anything I've ever seen. I remembered thinking, "This is why I picked up a camera in the first place—to photograph a place such as this." From several passages in Scripture, it is clear that the Lord took great delight in even the minutia of creation. I believe that God was directly involved with the generation and placement of every grain of sand, every drop of water, every canyon and cave, every mountain and meadow. Every little bit of the natural world is witness to the artistic eye of the Creator.

That's why I'm passionate about protecting the natural world and being a good steward of its beauty. True, some take "protecting the environment" to extremes. **But to disrespect the land is to respect the Divine Landowner. I've been to places of great natural beauty that were not stewarded properly, and the land suffered.**

That's why I am grateful for government agencies and private organizations that work to protect our public lands. The heavens and the earth testify to an invisible, masterful, and wondrous Creator; I want that testimony to sound forth for all time, and that's why I support protecting our public lands.

Late Afternoon Light
Monument Valley, Arizona

The Mittens & Merrick Butte
Monument Valley, Arizona

Photography has become a sort of cheap therapy for me. For fourteen years, I've wrestled with depression and grief since the sudden, unexpected death of my father. For the most part, I learned to live with it, but the sudden, unexpected death of my son just a few years ago compounded these maladies and rocked my faith. Spending time outdoors, chasing witness to the Creator through my viewfinder, I've begun to heal.

When God wanted to increase Abraham's faith, he beckoned the patriarch outdoors and said, "Look toward heaven, and number the stars" (Genesis 15:5). And when the Lord descended in a whirlwind to address Job's misery, he asked him. "Have you commanded the morning since your days began, and caused the dawn to know its place?" (Job 38:12).

All of the locations represented in this book are special to me, but Monument Valley in northeast Arizona is unlike anything else. In my three visits there, my sense of awe has increased each time, and I consider it "holy ground." I first visited in December 2008 and captured its beauty with a dusting of snow (opposite page). In April 2010, I brought my wife with me to experience the Valley's majesty.

But in September 2018, I made another pilgrimage to Tse'Bii'Ndzisgaii, as the Navajo call it, and again pointed my camera at the Mittens and Merrick Butte. I shot several panoramas, one in the very late afternoon as the sun cast its long shadows across the valley, and another the next morning. And I couldn't help but worship over what I saw.

I thought about my dad and my son. I thought about my grief and bitterness. I thought about the many angry tears I had shed. **But then I thought of Abraham and Job, and in the face of this blazing sunset, all of my bitterness melted like wax before the raging fire of Divine Glory. How can one remain bitter in the face of such beauty?** "The steadfast love of the LORD never ceases; his mercies never come to an end; they are new every morning; great is your faithfulness" (Lamentations 3:22-23).

Sunrise of Light & Fire
Monument Valley, Arizona

about the author

Michael Whitworth is an author, publisher, and seminar-speaker who calls Fort Worth, Texas his home. He also pursues landscape photography as an expensive hobby/cheap therapy (depending on your perspective).

When Michael is not writing, speaking, or snapping pictures, he enjoys reading, drinking coffee, and watching sports. He is a big fan of the Dallas Cowboys and Alabama Crimson Tide.

To see much more of Michael's photography, visit invisiblewitness.com.

www.ingramcontent.com/pod-product-compliance
Lightning Source LLC
Chambersburg PA
CBHW042108090526

44591CB00004B/44